**Genre** Realistic Fiction

## Essential Question

**How can we take responsibility?**

# Team Robot Ninja

by Peter Friend

illustrated by Francois Boutet

# Chapter 1 Mall Call

Mom and Dad were out grocery shopping. My big sister, Emma, was in her bedroom studying for some university exam. That left me to babysit my little brother, Oliver.

This wasn't a problem because although he was a couple of years younger than me, mostly we got along fine. I'd planned to hang out watching cartoons all afternoon anyway, so I figured we could do it together.

Then my cell phone rang, and everything changed.

"Cameron, I've got top-secret news: Benjamin Sato will be at Dragon Wings at five today," announced my good friend Maria.

"Do you mean *the* Benjamin Sato, the writer and director of *Team Robot Ninja*?"

"Of course that Benjamin Sato. How many Benjamin Satos do you know? Look, I'm coming over right now with my costume, and you should put yours on, too. We'll go together."

She hung up before I could say another word.

Maria and I were huge *Team Robot Ninja* fans. We thought it was the best *anime* TV series ever. I had the first two seasons on DVD, the complete set of collectible figurines (they took months of saving plus all my birthday money to afford), an official baseball cap, and two T-shirts.

Last year Maria and I both made costumes of our favorite characters. Naturally, I was Galaxorus Rex, the super-intelligent giant green lizard, and Maria was Hyper Shadow, the blue-haired alien telepath. Both costumes were pretty spectacular, not just your usual cardboard-and-duct-tape affairs. Gluing on the million or so lizard scales had taken me a whole week.

Just then my phone rang again. "Dude, have you heard?" came Tom's voice. "Benjamin Sato will be at—"

"Yeah, yeah, I heard," I interrupted him. "Maria and I are going, so if you want to come with us, be here in time for the 4:44 bus." As I put the phone down, I thought he probably wouldn't make it because that boy was late for everything.

Then my phone beeped with an incoming text message. It was Liz with the same "top-secret" news. I replied, telling her to meet us here.

I found my Galaxorus Rex costume in the back of the closet and wiped the dust from it. I wondered if I really wanted to walk around in public dressed as a giant lizard. On the other hand, maybe Benjamin Sato would pose for a photo with me if I wore it. I imagined a picture like that on my network page—epic!

Liz and Maria arrived, but Tom hadn't shown up (no surprise there). Maria changed into her Hyper Shadow costume, which looked fantastic, and then she and Liz nagged me to put on my costume too.

"Okay," I said with a sigh and headed to my bedroom.

I'd grown considerably in the last year, and the costume barely fit, but my reflection in the mirror still looked pretty cool. The girls cheered when I came back out. Oliver, who was still watching TV in the living room, yelled at us to shut up.

That's when it hit me—what would I do with Oliver?

"Hey, little brother," I said in my friendliest voice. "You want to come to the mall with us, don't you?"

"Not with you looking like a giant pickle," he replied.

I tried everything, even bribery with chocolate, but Oliver stood his ground, refusing to cooperate.

I suspected he was still sulking about my costume. I remembered that he'd wanted to borrow my Galaxorus Rex outfit for a costume party, but instead he'd had to go as a very unoriginal ghost in an old sheet with eyeholes cut in it.

"The bus leaves in five minutes," Liz said, glancing anxiously at the clock.

I couldn't let my bratty brother spoil my only chance to meet Benjamin Sato, right? Sure, I'd promised to babysit, but if you looked at things in proportion, this was far more important. Besides, it's not like I was leaving Oliver completely alone. Emma was still in the apartment.

"Hey, Emma, something really urgent came up. Can you babysit Oliver for a while?" I yelled down the hallway.

She shouted something back through her bedroom door.

"Thanks. Back soon," I yelled before she could change her mind, and then we raced out of the apartment.

"Where's Tom?" Maria asked.

"Late as always," I said. "Tough luck, but we can't wait."

# Chapter 2 Dragon Wings

Maria and I got weird looks on the bus. Two teenagers sniggered at us, and an old guy made some comment about the circus being in town. Maria wobbled her antennae and stared at him until he looked the other way.

I was glad the lizard head kept me hidden. No one could see me blushing or recognize my face. With Maria's blue wig and sunglasses, I doubted anyone recognized her either.

We reached the mall and found at least a hundred people lining up outside the Dragon Wings store: so much for top-secret news.

Several people were wearing *Team Robot Ninja* T-shirts or caps, but only Maria and I were in full costume. We got plenty more looks and comments, but mostly positive ones this time.

Then, looking around, I saw the scariest thing in the universe—my parents were walking straight toward us. I knew I was in terrible trouble.

I expected Mom and Dad to start shouting at me. I expected public humiliation and to be grounded until I was at least 25, but they sauntered past without a second glance.

Then I realized that they hadn't recognized me underneath the lizard costume. It was the perfect disguise.

I turned my attention back to the store. It was five o'clock, so why weren't they letting us in? I could see Benjamin Sato through the window, chatting with Mr. Angry, the store owner. (His real name is Anders, but everyone calls him Mr. Angry. Dragon Wings is the best comics and anime store in the city, but Mr. Angry seems to despise his customers.)

Finally Mr. Anders opened the door and glared at the crowd. "This is a business, not a charity for deadbeats and parasites. No one meets Mr. Sato without the official, authorized newspaper coupon," he announced.

About a hundred people groaned.

"Coupon, what coupon?" I asked Maria, who just shrugged.

"This is all your fault," Liz told me and stomped off.

A few customers smugly waved their coupons and skipped into the store, but most of the crowd left, grumbling as they departed. We were about to leave, too, when I heard, "Hey, Galaxorus Rex and Hyper Shadow!" It was Mr. Angry, and he was smiling at us. "Such great costumes deserve entry," he said.

Maria and I hurried inside the store before he could change his mind. Once inside, Mr. Angry introduced us to Benjamin Sato.

"Please, call me Ben," he said.

Then he and Mr. Angry raved about our costumes. Apparently, Mr. Angry was an even bigger *Team Robot Ninja* fan than we were.

We posed for tons of photos with Ben, and then he autographed our costumes and gave both of us a copy of the DVD for the third season.

I was having the best time ever when suddenly I realized that it was six o'clock and I'd been there a whole hour! I was ultra late and would have to leave right now or end up in serious trouble. Reluctantly, I said good-bye and headed for the door.

To my surprise, Maria followed me, so I told her that she could stay if she wanted to.

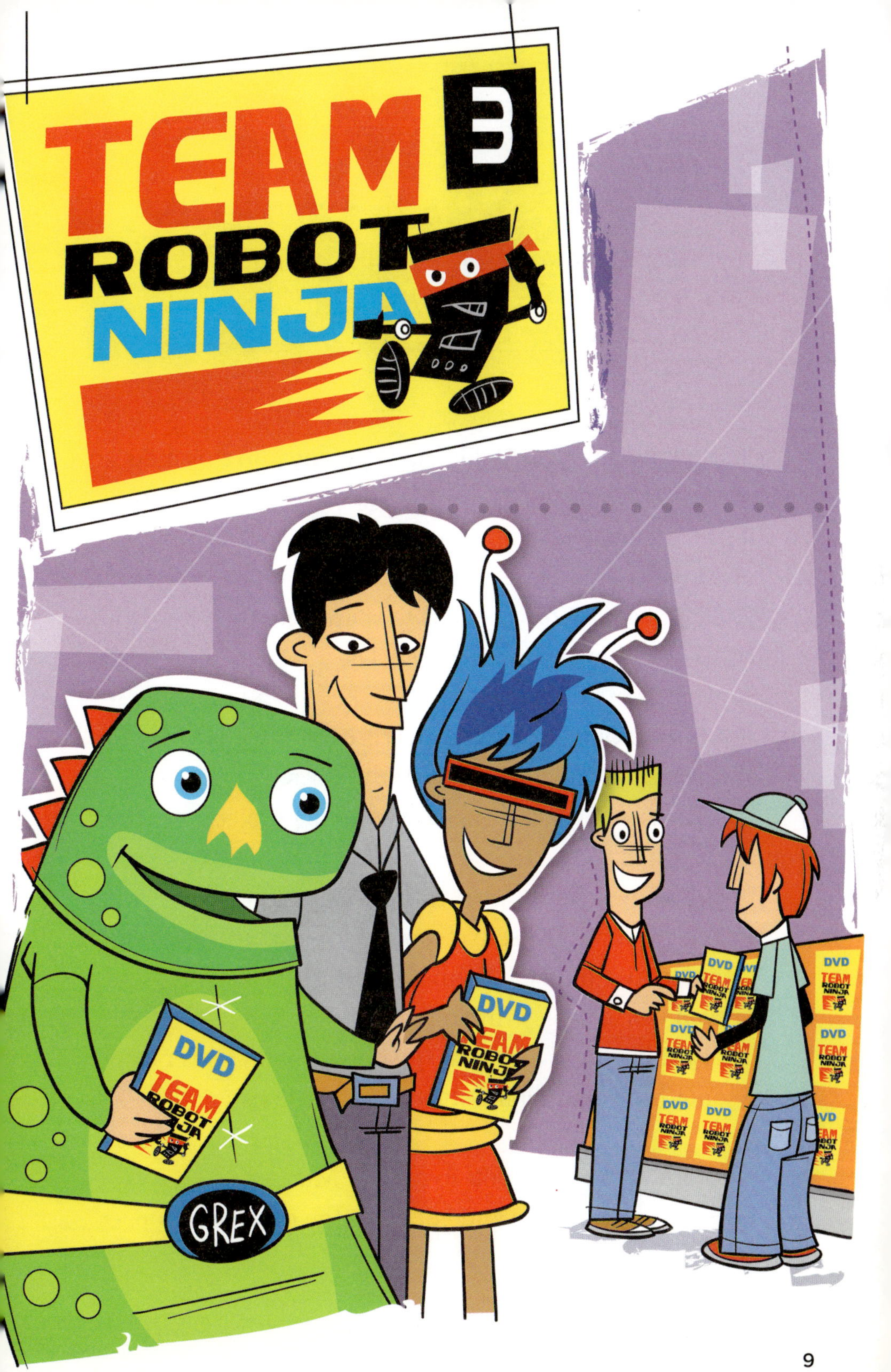
TEAM 3
ROBOT
NINJA
GREX
DVD
TEAM
ROBOT
NINJA

She explained that she had helped get me into this mess and that she felt an obligation to get me out of it.

"It's not really your fault," I replied as we began running to the bus stop, where we could see Liz waiting.

We caught a bus with seconds to spare, and then Maria and I showed Liz our autographs and DVDs.

"So where's my DVD?"

"Ben only gave us one each," Maria explained.

"You could've thought of me," Liz muttered.

"So, Cameron," Maria said, changing the subject, "what are you going to tell your parents?"

"I don't know what to say. I think they're going to be pretty angry with me for being so irresponsible."

"I think you should tell them the truth," she said. "Besides, it'll be even worse if they find out later."

"That's ridiculous," Liz said. "Just blame it on Oliver or make something up. I blame stuff on my little sister all the time."

"No wonder she hates you so much," Maria said.

"Losers," Liz muttered and got off at the following stop.

# Chapter 3 Telling the Truth

When we arrived home, my parents hadn't returned. I suspected I could get away with it after all, so I ran to my bedroom and pulled off my costume.

In the living room, Oliver was still watching television. To my amazement, Tom was sitting on the couch next to him.

"Hi, guys," Tom said, looking up. "When are we going to the mall?"

"We went more than an hour ago," I said, trying not to sound too critical.

Tom explained that he hadn't been able to find us, so he'd decided to keep Oliver company instead.

Oliver poked his tongue out at me and then said, "Tom's my new big brother."

Oliver was right—Tom had been a better brother than I had—which made me feel terrible.

Tom and Maria left just as Mom and Dad arrived home.

Dad thanked me for taking care of Oliver, and I half expected Oliver to spill the beans at the top of his voice, but when I looked over, he was engrossed in watching a local television news report. Maria and I were on the screen, posing beside Benjamin Sato at Dragon Wings.

"That costume's much better than your ridiculous one," Oliver told me haughtily.

Seriously, he didn't recognize me on the television? I knew then that he hadn't even noticed I'd left the apartment.

"Oh, that must be the gathering we saw at the mall," Mom said. "Look, Phillip, it's those animal things Cameron likes."

"Mm-hmm," Dad said, not particularly interested.

My parents didn't recognize Maria and me in our costumes either.

"Hey," Emma said, wandering in from the kitchen with a soda in her hand.

"Well, if it isn't our industrious daughter," Dad replied. "I hope you got lots of studying done and your dear sweet brothers weren't too much trouble?"

"Actually, the boys behaved better than usual," she said, sounding surprised. "They were a bit boisterous around four-thirty, but they quieted down when I yelled at them through the door."

I realized that Emma hadn't heard what I said before I went and that she didn't know I'd left the apartment either. It was unbelievable—no one knew. I was answerable to no one, which made me the luckiest kid ever, right?

So why did I feel so bad?

Although no one in my family realized it, I knew I was a terrible brother. Even Tom, the guy who's late to everything and forgets what day it is, was a better brother to Oliver than I was that afternoon.

My conscience was hurting. I knew Maria had been right—it would be awful if my actions were found out later, and I knew it would be even worse if the guilt hung over me for all eternity.

As for Liz, I sure didn't want to turn into someone like her. I took a deep breath, pointed to the television screen, and said, "Uh, that's me."

My family looked at the screen with puzzled expressions.

I explained that I had gone to the mall that afternoon to meet Benjamin Sato and had left Oliver alone.

"I'm really sorry because I promised I'd babysit Oliver, and I broke my promise," I added.

"I'm not a baby!" shouted Oliver indignantly.

"And I'm sorry, Oliver, for abandoning you," I said.

"Tom was here, and he's more fun than you anyway."

"Yeah, well, good, but I can't take any credit for that. I didn't know he'd be here. I'm sorry to you too, Emma, because I should have gone to your room to talk to you instead of just yelling down the hallway. Of course, I should have taken responsibility for Oliver myself anyway, like I said I would."

"That's true, and I think you owe Tom an apology too," Mom said. "That's no way to treat your friends."

"Yeah, I guess I do. I'll go and see him after dinner, and I'll lend him my new *Team Robot Ninja* DVD."

"He'll have to come and pick it up," Dad said, "because you're grounded for the next five years."

"But at least you told us the truth," Mom continued. "Maybe we'll give you a couple of years off for good behavior."

After dinner, and washing and drying the dishes all by myself without being asked, I went to my bedroom. My Galaxorus Rex costume lay on my bed, staring back at me. It looked miserable somehow, with its side seams all ripped where I'd over-stretched it that afternoon.

Just then Oliver appeared at my side. "Cheer up, Cameron. I'll watch *Team Robot Ninja* with you," he said generously.

I thanked Oliver and asked him if he wanted to try on the costume.

"What, are you giving it to me?"

"It's way cooler than your ghost costume. Let's see if it needs any adjustments," I told him.

When the pants fell down, I tried not to laugh. "Don't worry about it. We'll add some elastic when we repair the seams," I said.

Oliver nodded, admiring himself in the mirror. "We can fix it up together, can't we, Cameron?"

I smiled because things had turned out pretty well after all.

# Respond to Reading

## Summarize

Use important details from *Team Robot Ninja* to summarize how Cameron took responsibility for his actions. Information from your graphic organizer may help you.

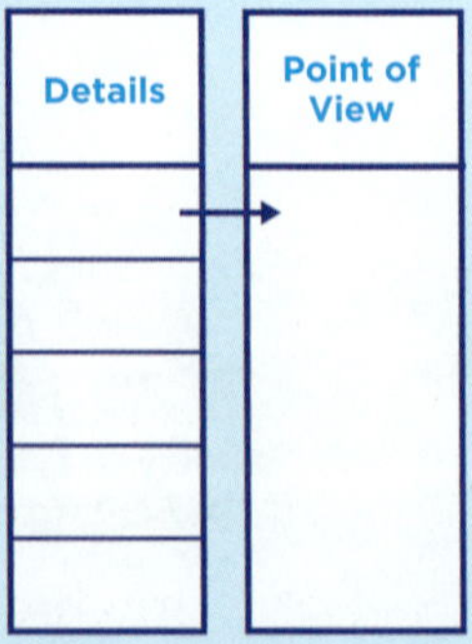


## Text Evidence

1. What features tell you this is realistic fiction? **GENRE**

2. The story is told from Cameron's point of view. How does this help you to understand how he feels about the events that take place in the story? **POINT OF VIEW**

3. What is the meaning of "on the other hand" on page 4? What clues in the text helped you to figure this out? **IDIOMS**

4. Write about whether using the first-person point of view in this story is an effective way to tell the story. Include examples from the text to support your answer. **WRITE ABOUT READING**

**Genre** Poetry

## Compare Texts

Read a poem about Cameron's changing relationship with his brother Oliver.

# Game On!

Sitting around the apartment,
Grounded for another thousand hours,
So bored my brain's about to burst.
I've even done my homework
When Oliver arrives.
"Hey, older brother," he grins and delivers
*Team Robot Ninja*, the video game, into my hungry hands.
Yay, hooray. High five, high ten.
"Let's play," he says.
Oh.
You see, Oliver's no great gamer, not even good.
He's a slow mover, a joystick jolter, a miserable loser.
But still, I promised
To be a better brother,
And besides, I'm really bored. (Did I mention that before?)

So we play.
Level One's fun,
Racing a hovercraft over the ochre Martian desert,
Collecting colored crystals
To feed the sand snakes before they feed on us.

Level Two's cool, too.
We chase bank robbers through an airport lounge,
Dodging vampire bats and baseball caps.
(Who writes these games?)

But Level Three is hard,
A platform puzzler with trick bricks and spinning blades.
"Aaaaargh!" Oliver yells
As we fail to make it for the hundredth time.
Here comes the tantrum, I think, but
"Got it," he says.
"You stand on the trapdoor and stop the giant spider
While I climb the rope to flip the switch."
And he's absolutely right.

Illustration: Francois Boutet

Level Four takes us four days to finish.
We don't care—we're having fun.
"You're not such a bad brother after all," Oliver tells me.
"Same to you," I say.
"We should try *Super Sword* or *Clone Zone*,
Games you used to be too young for."
"I'm a year older than I was a year ago," he insists.
Well, yeah, that's true.
"And I'll help you make your new *Team* costume," he says.
"Oh," I say, remembering his past disasters—
Glue in the hair,
Blue paint on the stairs,
Whining and tears.
Trying to be kinder, I say,
"Thanks." Sighing inside.
It's not easy being the perfect brother.

## Make Connections

In *Game On!*, what responsibilities does Cameron find are involved with being a good brother? **ESSENTIAL QUESTION**

Compare the attitude of Liz toward her younger sister in *Team Robot Ninja* with Cameron's attitude toward Oliver in *Game On!* when something goes wrong. **TEXT TO TEXT**

Illustration: François Boulet

# Focus on Literary Elements

**Alliteration** *Game On!* is a free-verse poem that explores the theme of responsibility for being a good brother. In free verse, there is no regular rhyme scheme, although the poet may add a rhyme from time to time. In free verse, the poet can use other ways to create rhythm and energy. Alliteration is one way to do this. Alliteration means the poet repeats the first sound in a group of words; for example, "Peter Piper picked a peck of pickled peppers."

**Read and Find** In a number of places in *Game On!*, the poet has used alliteration with groups of words. For example, on page 17, the poet repeatedly uses the sound of *b* in "So bored my brain's about to burst" and "But still, I promised to be a better brother, and besides, I'm really bored." On page 19, the poet uses the letter *s* in the same way: "'Same to you,' I say. 'We should try *Super Sword* ...'" Each example of alliteration creates a rhythm that gives energy to the free-verse form of the poem.

## Your Turn

Choose an event, person, or object and write a short free-verse poem explaining your thoughts and feelings. In several places in the poem, include an example of alliteration. Now read your poem aloud to a partner. Ask your partner to identify each example of alliteration as he or she listens to you read.